JOY IN THE JOURNEY

Leisure Arts, Inc. • Maumelle Arkansas

Table of Contents

There is a time for
everything and a
season for every
activity under heaven
ECC. 3:1

The Lord is my shepherd

Blessings
to the little
bee
that brings us
nectar
for our tea

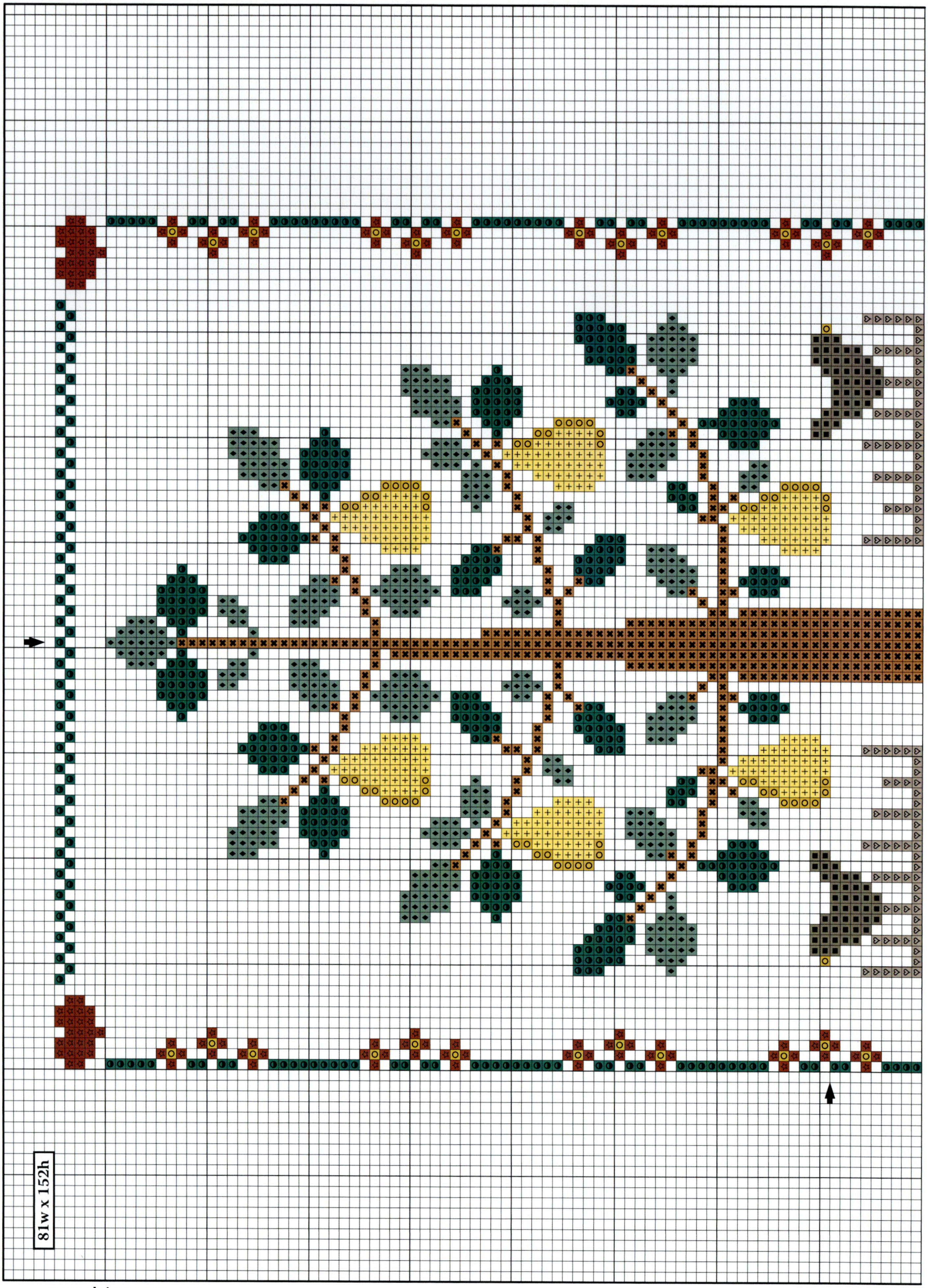
81w x 152h

EVERY GOOD TREE (81w x 152h)

X	DMC	ANC.	COLOR	MH#
▢	ecru	387	ecru	
☆	300	352	rust	
✖	420	374	brown	
▽	644	830	beige	
+	676	891	lt gold	62041
O	729	890	gold	62031
▽	3045	888	lt brown	

X	DMC	B'ST	ANC.	COLOR
◒	3051		681	green
◆	3052	⁄	262	lt green
■	3787		273	grey
●	3052		262	lt green Fr. Knot

▢ Grey area indicates last row of top section of design.

We used Mill Hill beads in place of floss for pears.

Every Good Tree (81w x 152h)

14 count	5⅞"	x	10⅞"
16 count	5⅛"	x	9½"
18 count	4½"	x	8½"

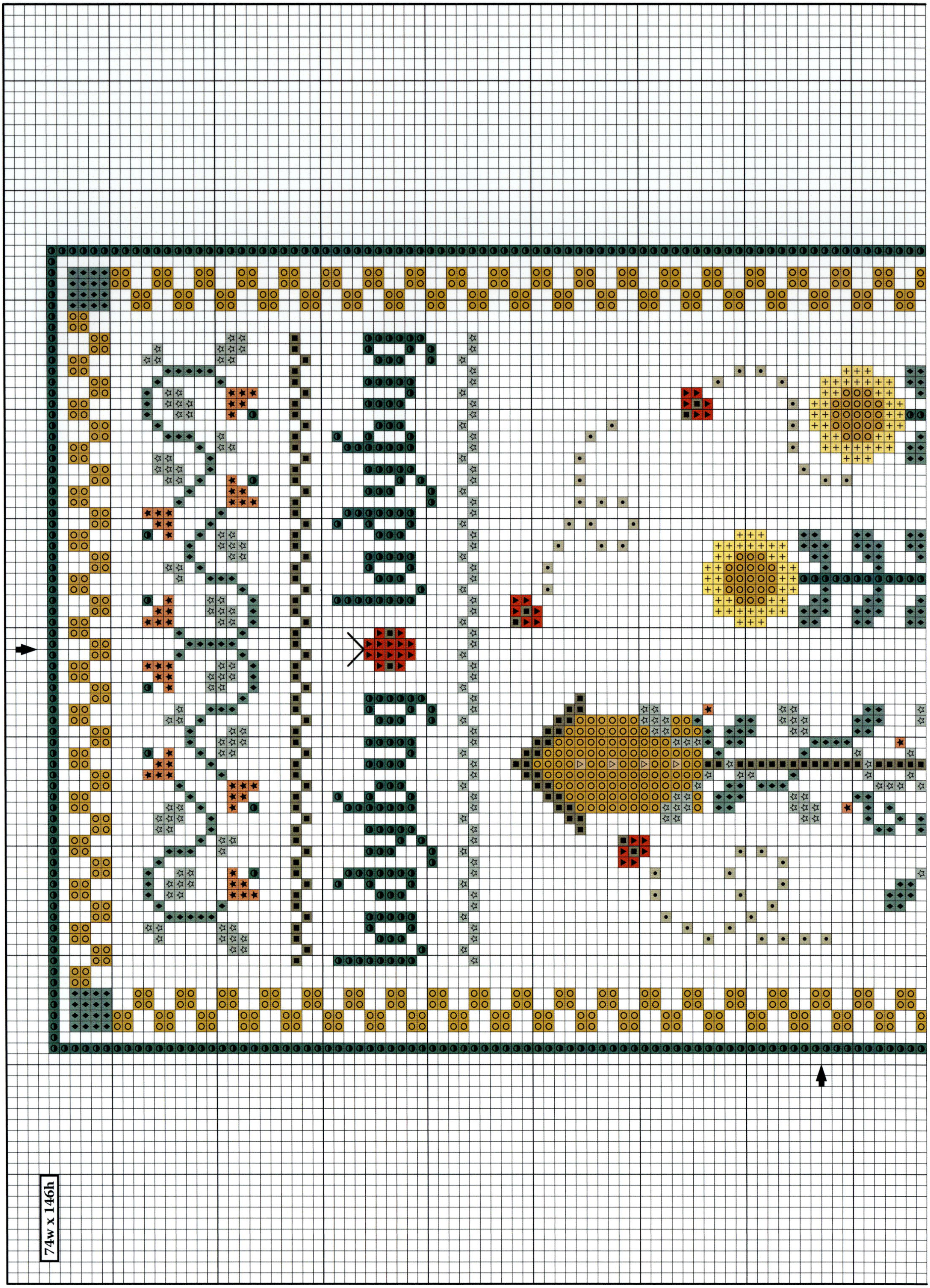
74w x 146h

LADYBUG (74w x 146h)

X	DMC	ANC.	COLOR	MH#
▽	422	943	tan	62031
○	780	309	gold	62023
+	782	307	lt gold	62031
◒	935	861	dk green	
•	3032	903	lt grey	
◆	3051	681	green	
☆	3052	262	lt green	
▼	3777	1015	red	62032

X	DMC	B'ST	ANC.	COLOR	MH#
■	3787	/	273	grey	03009
★	3830		5975	lt red	62013

Grey area indicates last row of top section of design.

We used Mill Hill beads in place of floss for flowers, hearts, strawberries, & large ladybug. Ladybug charms were used in place of floss for each small ladybug.

Ladybug (74w x 146h)

14 count	5⅜"	x	10½"
16 count	4⅝"	x	9⅛"
18 count	4⅛"	x	8⅛"

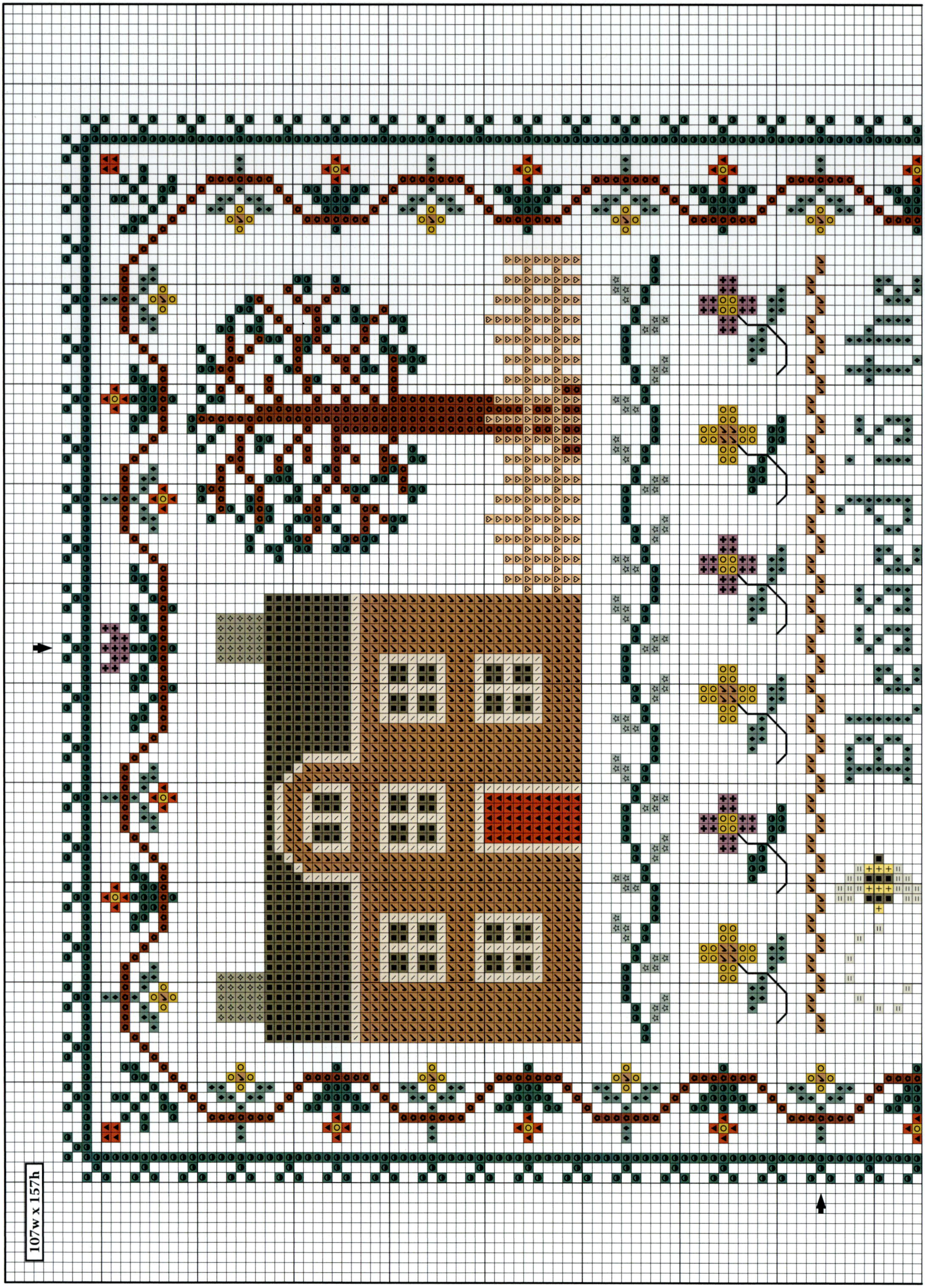
107w x 157h

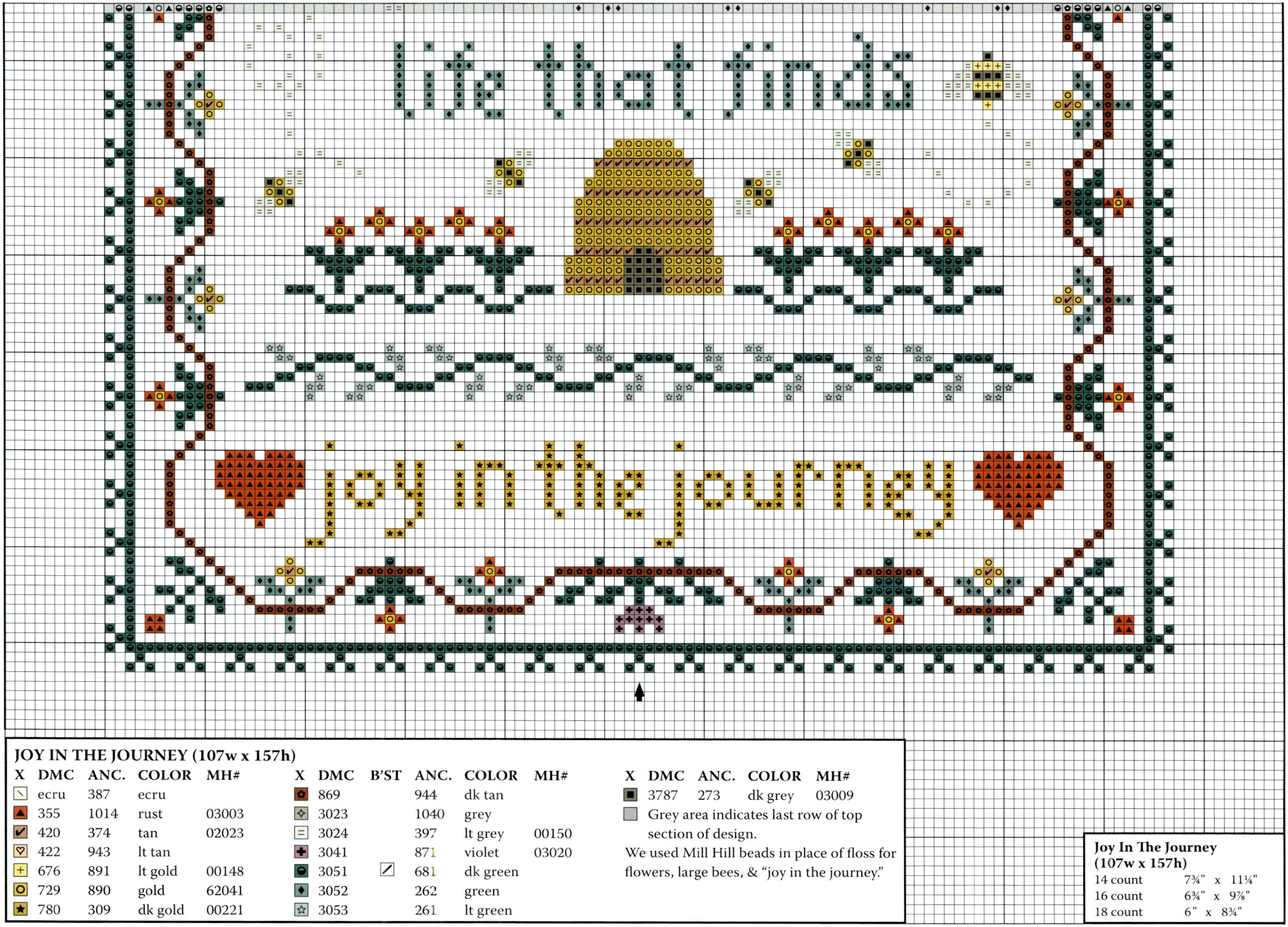

JOY IN THE JOURNEY (107w x 157h)

X	DMC	B'ST	ANC.	COLOR	MH#
	ecru		387	ecru	
	355		1014	rust	03003
	420		374	tan	02023
	422		943	lt tan	
	676		891	lt gold	00148
	729		890	gold	62041
	780		309	dk gold	00221
	869		944	dk tan	
	3023		1040	grey	
	3024		397	lt grey	00150
	3041		871	violet	03020
	3051	/	681	dk green	
	3052		262	green	
	3053		261	lt green	
	3787		273	dk grey	03009

Grey area indicates last row of top section of design.

We used Mill Hill beads in place of floss for flowers, large bees, & "joy in the journey."

Joy In The Journey
(107w x 157h)

14 count	7¾"	x	11¼"
16 count	6¾"	x	9⅞"
18 count	6"	x	8¾"

Every good tree
MT 7:17
bears good fruit

There is a time for everything and a season for every activity under heaven
ECC. 3:1
The Lord is my shepherd

Blessed is the
life that finds
joy in the journey

ladybug ladybug
fly away home
Blessings
to the little
bee
that brings us
nectar
for our tea

There is a time for
everything and a
season for every
87w x 155h

THERE IS A TIME (87w x 155h)

X	DMC	ANC.	COLOR
⟍	ecru	387	ecru
✿	221	897	red
✔	420	374	brown
8	434	310	dk tan
4	435	1046	tan

X	DMC	B'ST	ANC.	COLOR
2	437		362	lt tan
✧	3023		1040	lt grey
✚	3041		871	violet
●	3051		681	dk green
◆	3052	⟋	262	green

X	DMC	ANC.	COLOR
■	3053	261	lt green
☆	3787	273	grey
•	3052	262	green Fr. Knot
▒	Grey area indicates last row of top section of design.		

There Is A Time (87w x 155h)

14 count	6¼"	x 11⅛"
16 count	5½"	x 9¾"
18 count	4⅞"	x 8⅝"

107w x 107h

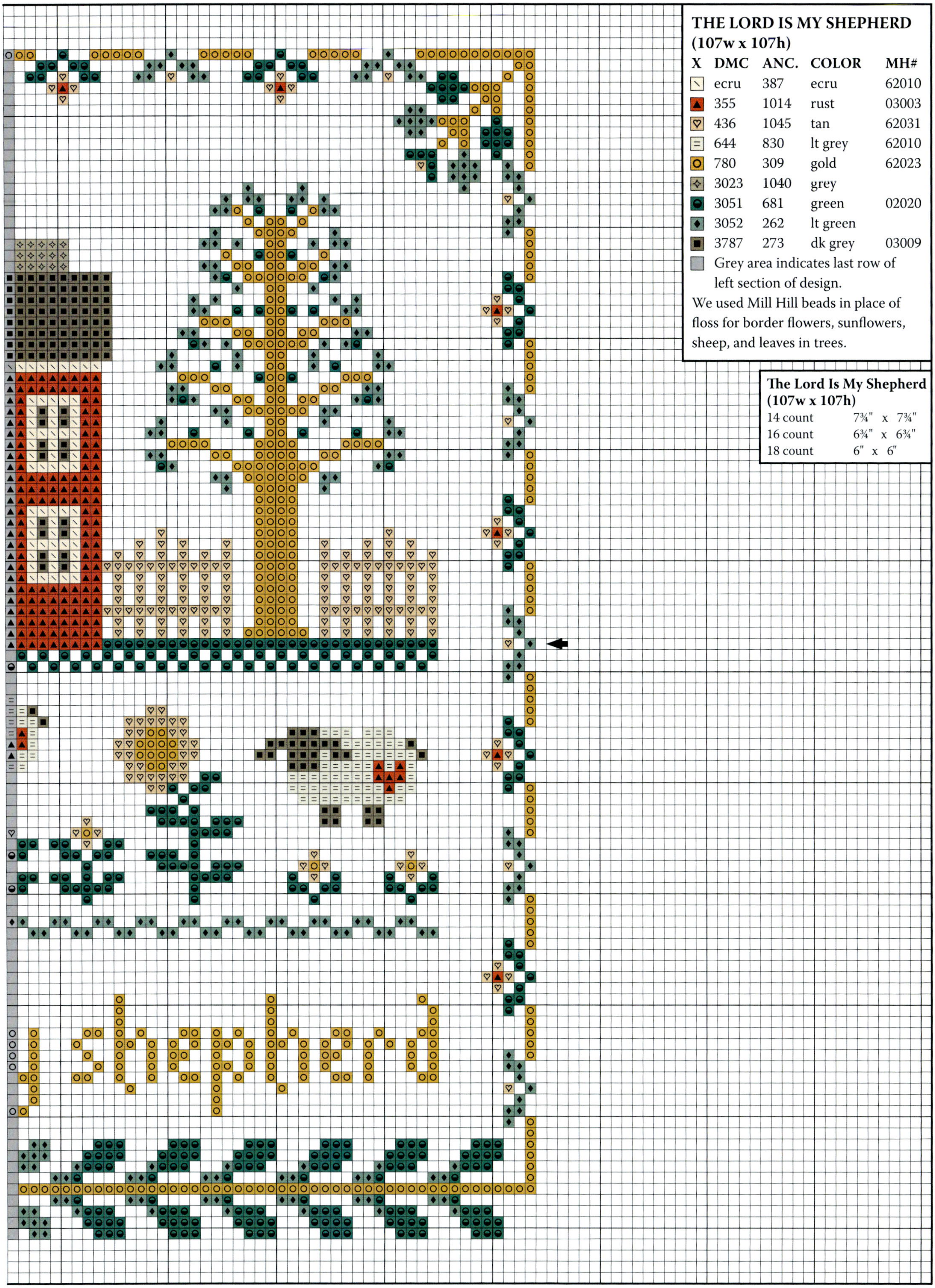

THE LORD IS MY SHEPHERD
(107w x 107h)

X	DMC	ANC.	COLOR	MH#
	ecru	387	ecru	62010
	355	1014	rust	03003
	436	1045	tan	62031
	644	830	lt grey	62010
	780	309	gold	62023
	3023	1040	grey	
	3051	681	green	02020
	3052	262	lt green	
	3787	273	dk grey	03009

Grey area indicates last row of left section of design.

We used Mill Hill beads in place of floss for border flowers, sunflowers, sheep, and leaves in trees.

The Lord Is My Shepherd
(107w x 107h)

14 count	7¾" x 7¾"
16 count	6¾" x 6¾"
18 count	6" x 6"

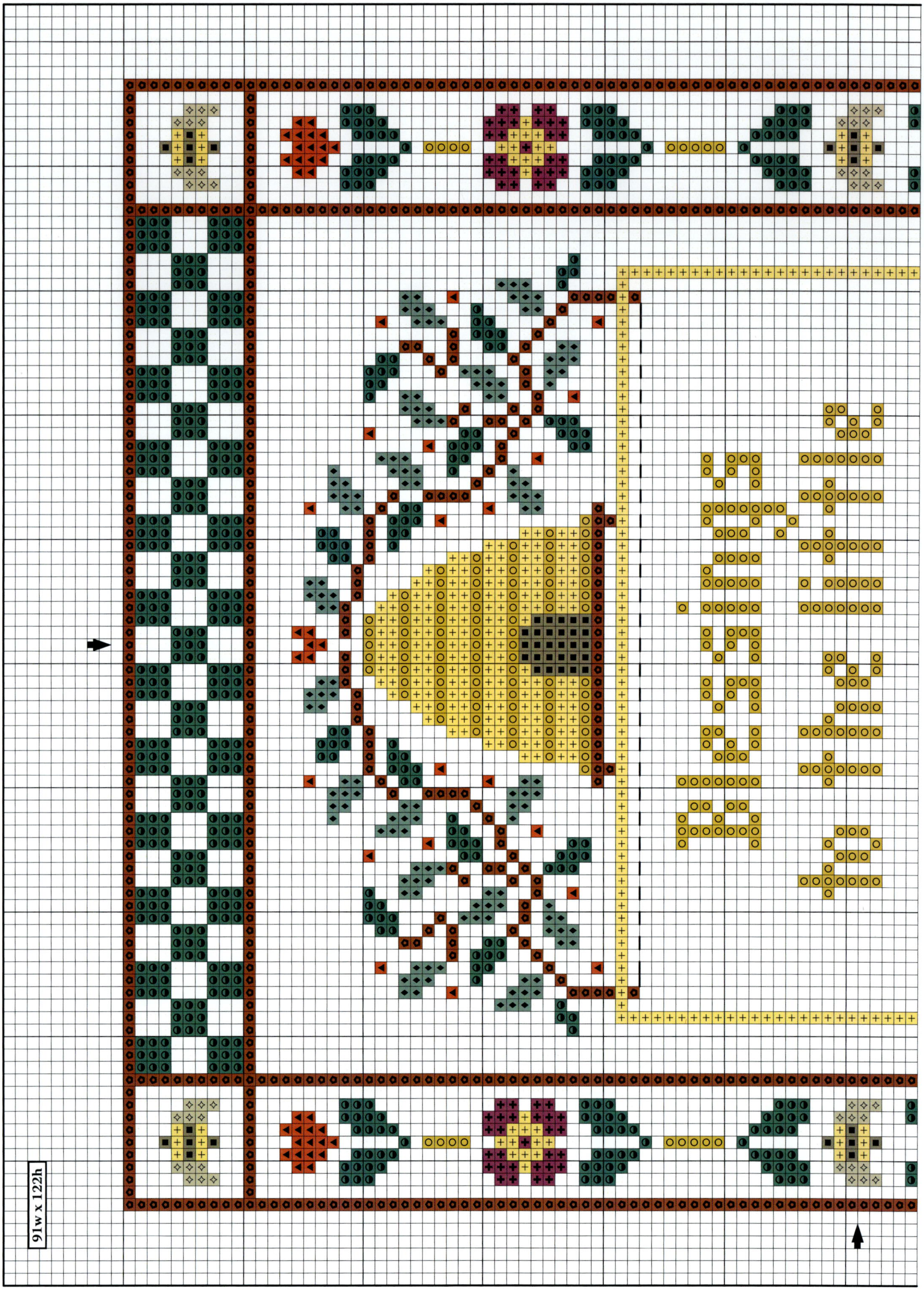
91w x 122h

BLESSINGS TO THE BEE (91w x 122h)

X	DMC	B'ST	ANC.	COLOR
✚	327		100	purple
✿	433	⁄	358	brown
+	729		890	lt gold
O	780		309	gold
✓	841		1082	beige

X	DMC	ANC.	COLOR	MH#
▲	918	341	rust	03003
✧	3024	397	lt grey	
◒	3051	681	green	
◆	3052	262	lt green	
■	3787	273	grey	

Grey area indicates last row of top section of design.

We used Mill Hill beads in place of floss for heart & flowers surrounding beehive.

We used a bee charm in place of floss for each corner bee.

Blessings To The Bee (91w x 122h)

14 count	6½"	x 8¾"
16 count	5¾"	x 7⅝"
18 count	5⅛"	x 6⅞"

Heart And Home
(57w x 62h)

14 count	4⅛"	x	4½"
16 count	3⅝"	x	3⅞"
18 count	3¼"	x	3½"

HEART AND HOME
(57w x 62h)

X	DMC	ANC.	COLOR
⟍	ecru	387	ecru
✖	420	374	brown
○	783	306	gold
●	3051	681	dk green
◆	3052	262	green
☆	3053	261	lt green
▼	3777	1015	red
■	3787	273	grey

General Instructions

Project Information

All designs were stitched on 14 count Antique White Aida. In some designs, Mill Hill beads or charms were used in place of floss as noted in color key. Two strands of floss were used for Cross Stitch, Backstitch, French Knots, beads, and charms. The designs were custom framed.

How to Read Charts

Each chart is made up of a key and a gridded design where each square represents a stitch. The symbols in the key tell which floss color to use for each stitch in the chart. The following headings and symbols are given:

X - Cross Stitch
DMC - DMC color number
B'ST- Backstitch
ANC. - Anchor color number
Color - the name given to the floss color in this chart
MH# - Mill Hill bead color number

A square filled with a color and a symbol should be worked as a **Cross Stitch.**

A straight line should be worked as a **Backstitch**.

A large dot listed near the end of the key should be worked as a **French Knot**.

In the chart, the symbol for a **Cross Stitch** may be omitted or reduced when a **Backstitch** crosses its square.

How to Stitch

Always work Cross Stitches first and then add the Backstitch and French Knots.

Cross Stitch (X): For horizontal rows, work stitches in two journeys ***(Fig. 1)***. For vertical rows, complete each stitch as shown ***(Fig. 2)***. When working over two fabric threads, work Cross Stitch as shown in Fig. 3.

Fig. 1

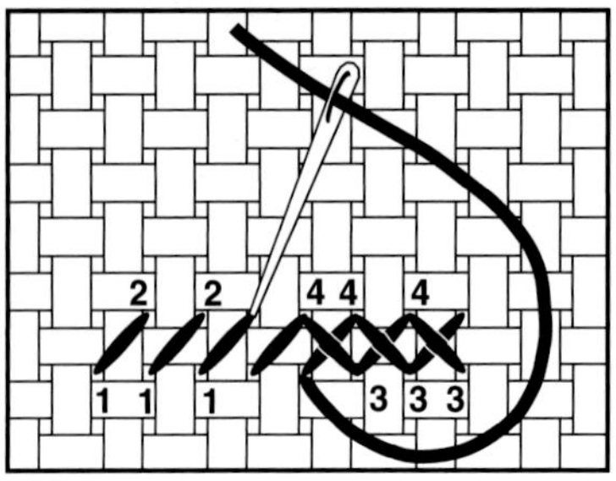

Fig. 2

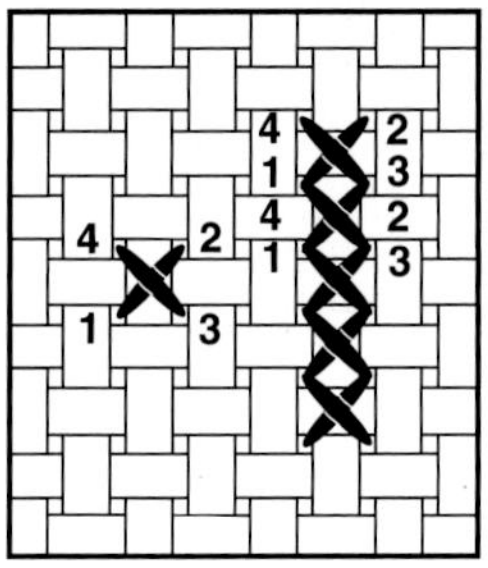

Fig. 3

Backstitch (B'ST): For outlines and details, Backstitch should be worked after the design has been completed ***(Fig. 4)***. When working over two fabric threads, work Backstitch as shown in ***Fig. 5***.

Fig. 4

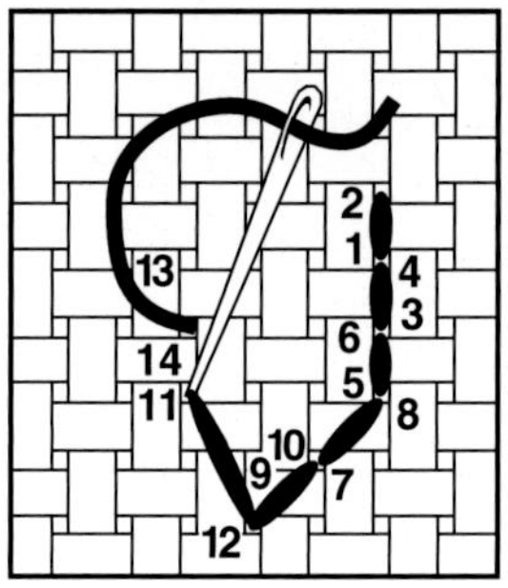

Fig. 5

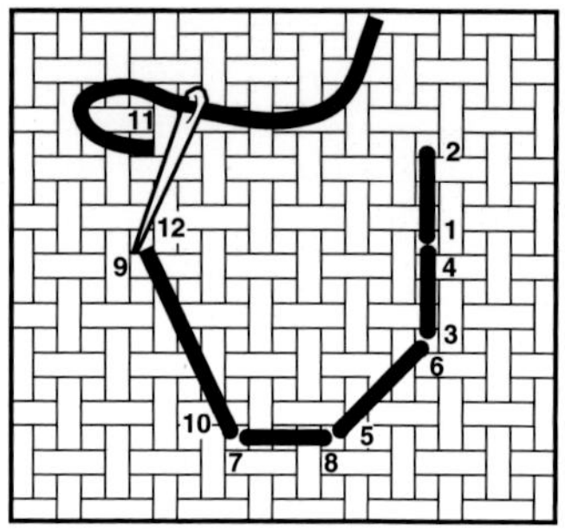

French Knot: Bring needle up at 1. Wrap floss once around needle. Insert needle at 2, tighten knot, and pull needle through fabric, holding floss until it must be released ***(Fig. 6)***. For a larger knot, use more floss strands; wrap only once.

Fig. 6

Stitching Tips

Preparing Fabric

Being sure to allow plenty of margin, cut fabric desired size and overcast raw edges. It is better to waste a little fabric than to come up short after hours of stitching!

Working with Floss

To ensure smoother stitches, separate strands and realign them before threading needle. Keep stitching tension consistent. Begin and end floss by running under several stitches on back; never tie knots.

Where to Start

The horizontal and vertical centers of each charted design are shown by arrows. You may start at any point on the charted design, but be sure the design will be centered on the fabric. Locate the center of fabric by folding in half, top to bottom and again left to right. On the charted design, count the number of squares (stitches) from the center of the chart to where you wish to start. Then from the fabric's center, find your starting point by counting out the same number of fabric threads (stitches).

Attaching Beads: To sew bead in place, use 2 strands of floss and a fine needle that will pass through bead. Secure floss on back of fabric. Bring needle up through fabric, run needle through bead, and back down through fabric ***(Fig. 7)***. Continue to add beads in this manner until beaded area is complete. Secure floss on back of fabric.

Fig. 7

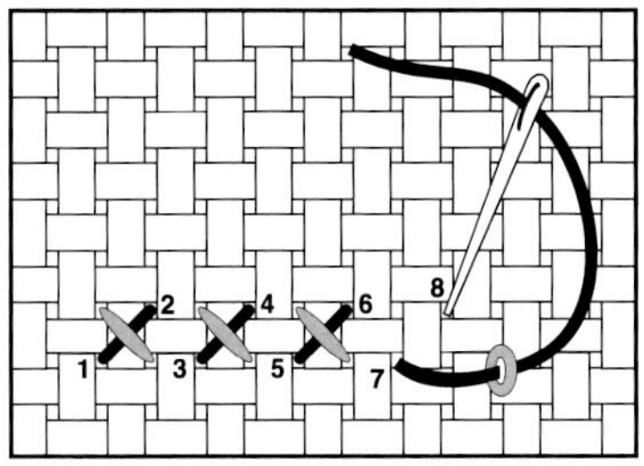

We have made every effort to ensure that these instructions are accurate and complete. We cannot, however, be responsible for human error, typographical mistakes, or variations in individual work.

Made in U.S.A.

Show us what you’re working on!

Share your project photos with us on social media.
Tag us @leisureartsinc or use #leisurearts